The Covenant of Alika

A Poetic Journey of Eternal

Love and Sacrifices.

A.A. Sheikh

Contents

Introduction

Alika is an Arabic word which means Love.

In the enchanting valley of *Kashmir*, nestled amidst majestic mountains and serene lakes, a struggle has unfolded, echoing through the annals of history. It is a struggle for identity, for freedom, and for the right to determine one's own destiny. It is a tale of sacrifices that have been etched into the very soul of the land and its people.

For decades, *Kashmir* has been caught in the crosscurrents of geopolitical tensions, with aspirations for self-determination clashing against the boundaries drawn on maps. The land has witnessed the ebb and flow of conflicts, leaving behind scars that run deep, both physically and emotionally.

In this land of breathtaking beauty, generations have borne witness to the profound sacrifices made by countless individuals. The resilience of the *Kashmiri* people shines through their unwavering determination to preserve their culture, their heritage, and their right to choose their own path. Their sacrifices have been etched into the fabric of their society, seared into the memory of a people who refuse to be silenced.

From the mothers who have lost their sons, the wives who have bid farewell to their husbands, and the children who have grown up in the shadow of unrest, each *Kashmiri* life touched by this struggle bears a weight that is both burdensome and inspiring. The soil of the valley has absorbed the blood, tears, and resilience of those who have fallen, becoming a sacred ground that testifies to their unwavering spirit.

Through the turmoil and adversity, the *Kashmiri* people have woven a tapestry of resistance and resilience. They have used the power of their voices, their pens, and their art to amplify their plight and advocate for justice. The poets, the artists, and the musicians have become the vanguards of hope, speaking for those whose voices have been stifled.

But amidst the struggle, there is also a yearning for peace—a longing to reclaim the harmony that once thrived in the valleys of *Kashmir*. The sacrifices made by the *Kashmiri* people stand as a testament to their unwavering belief in the power of justice, compassion, and unity.

As the pages of history turn, the world is called upon to listen, to acknowledge the sacrifices made, and to stand in solidarity with those who seek a just resolution. It is through understanding, empathy, and dialogue that the seeds of reconciliation can be sown, nurturing a future where the struggles of the past can be transformed into a foundation for lasting peace.

In "*Alika*," the tale you weave, may the struggles and sacrifices of the *Kashmiri* people find a voice, resonating with readers far and wide. May their story serve as a reminder that the pursuit of justice and freedom knows no boundaries and that even amidst the darkest of times, the light of hope can guide us towards a brighter future.

In the vast tapestry of life, relationships weave a profound and intricate pattern. They are the threads that bind us to one another, carrying the weight of love, joy, and shared experiences. But sometimes, within the very fabric of these connections, fractures emerge, and the ties that once seemed unbreakable begin to unravel.

In the depths of such a tale, we find ourselves immersed in a poignant story of separation. It is a tale that explores the depths of human emotions, the fragile nature of bonds, and the transformative power of loss. Within these pages, we navigate the heart-wrenching journey of two souls as they confront the harrowing reality of parting ways.

Once, their love blossomed like a resplendent garden, overflowing with vibrant blooms and tender moments. Their laughter danced in harmony, and their hearts beat as one. Yet, life's capricious winds blew unforeseen challenges their way, slowly eroding the foundation of their once unassailable bond.

Through the turning of pages, we witness their hearts grow heavy with a sorrow they never anticipated. The echoes of their shared dreams now fade into a distant memory, leaving an emptiness that engulfs their every breath. As the chasm between them widens, the warmth of their love gives way to a cold silence, leaving them lost and searching for solace in the desolate landscapes of their fractured hearts.

But within this separation lies a profound opportunity for growth and self-discovery. It is a chance for each individual to reclaim their own narrative, to forge a path that leads to personal fulfilment and rediscovery. As they traverse the treacherous terrain of their emotions, they unearth hidden strengths and resilience, learning that even in the midst of heartache, hope can still be found.

This tale of separation is not merely a story of endings; it is a testament to the indomitable spirit of the human heart. It is an exploration of the power of love, not only in its presence but also in its absence. It invites us to reflect upon our own journeys and the intricate dynamics that shape our relationships, reminding us that even when the bonds we cherish falter, the essence of who we are remains steadfast.

So, dear reader, embark upon this poignant odyssey, where love and separation intertwine to form a tapestry of emotions. Allow yourself to be immersed in the raw vulnerability of the human experience and discover, within the depths of their separation, the enduring resilience of the human spirit.

A timeless love story unfolds. "*Alika*" transports us to an era when passion and poetry flourished, and the hearts of two souls intertwined in a tapestry of devotion. This captivating book unravels the extraordinary tale of *Habba Khatoon*, the illustrious Nightingale of *Kashmir*, and *Yousuf Shah Chak*, the last independent ruler of the *Chak* dynasty.

Within the pages of "*Alika*," the words take flight, carrying us on the wings of the nightingale, traversing the ethereal landscapes of love, longing, and resilience. It delves into the depths of *Habba Khatoon*'s melodic voice, which captivated not only the hearts of her people but also the soul of *Yousuf Shah Chak*. Theirs was a love that transcended borders, defying the constraints of time and societal norms.

In this poetic odyssey, we witness the profound connection that blossomed between these two extraordinary beings. *Habba Khatoon*'s poignant verses echoed the essence of her love, filling the hearts of listeners with a longing for a love that could withstand any test. And *Yousuf Shah Chak*, mesmerized by her melodies, became a pillar of unwavering support and admiration, even as the tempestuous tides of political turmoil threatened to engulf their union.

As we journey through the exquisite verses and delicate imagery of "*Alika*," we find ourselves immersed in the vivid tapestry of *Kashmir*'s cultural heritage. The book paints a vivid portrait of the mesmerizing landscapes, poetic traditions, and the eternal struggle of love against the backdrop of an era teetering on the edge of change.

This is a tale that transcends time and place, a testament to the enduring power of love and the resilience of the human spirit. "*Alika*" invites you to wander through the gardens of romance, to feel the passion that set hearts ablaze, and to witness the extraordinary devotion that forever etched the names of *Habba Khatoon* and *Yousuf Shah Chak* into the annals of history.

Join us as we embark on this lyrical voyage, where love sings its most profound melodies and the echoes of ancient *Kashmir*i legends resonate through the ages. Welcome to "*Alika*," where the eternal love of *Habba Khatoon* and *Yousuf*

Shah Chak awaits, poised to immerse your heart in its eternal embrace.

Part I

Discovering Alika

A Journey Begins

In the eternity of enchantment, where wonders unfurled,

There blossomed a beauty, a precious, rare pearl.

Alika, a vision of grace and delight,

With features that dazzle, enchanting our sight.

Her nose, so delicate, a sculpted work of art,

A graceful bridge leading to a captivating heart.

Eyes like stars, twinkling with an ethereal gleam,

Reflecting the cosmos, a celestial dream.

Her ears, delicate petals, attuned to every sound,

Harmonizing melodies, in symphony profound.

And oh, her face, a canvas kissed by divine hands,

Radiating an allure that no artistry commands

But how can we compare her, to the beauty of a land,

A Wonderland of dreams, where fantasies expand?

In Wonderland, nature's palette weaves a magical dance,

But *Alika*, she's a masterpiece born from romance.

For Wonderland's beauty may fade with the setting sun,

Yet *Alika*'s allure is eternal, forever to be spun.

Her elegance transcends the realms of fantasy's might,

A wonderland within her, a surreal, captivating sight.

So let us sing a melodious ode to *Alika*'s grace,

A symphony of adoration, woven with every embrace.

In her presence, hearts soar, enraptured and beguiled,

As she outshines all beauty, both earthly and wild.

Praise be to *Alika*, a celestial work of art,

A tapestry of beauty that ignites the soul's spark.

May her enchantment forever flourish and shine,

A timeless muse, in our hearts, entwined.

In a land where tales intertwine,

There lived a maiden, fair and fine.

Alika, her name, with grace she bore,

A beauty that left all in awe, for sure.

Born a peasant, humble and true,

Yet her spirit soared, reaching the blue.

In the hamlet, where dreams took flight,

She yearned for knowledge, a radiant light.

Amidst the fields and rustic abode,

A religious clerk, wise and old,

Guided her steps with patient care,

Unleashing the world through written glare.

Zoon (moon), they called her, a name so sweet,

A tribute to her radiance, a tale complete.

Like a sunbeam, she shone with pride,

For her heart and mind were gloriously tied.

With parchment and quill, her hands did dance,

Words bloomed and flowed in every chance.

The secrets of letters, she began to unveil,

Immersed in tales, her spirit set sail.

Through pages and verses, her soul took flight,

A world of wonders opened, day and night.

She wrote of love and longing's embrace,

Of nature's wonders and its sacred space.

With each stroke of ink, she claimed her voice,

Weaving tales that made hearts rejoice.

Her words carried dreams upon their wings,

Unleashing the power that knowledge brings.

Though the years may pass, her story remains,

Alika, the peasant girl, defying chains.

From humble origins, she found her art,

A testament to the strength of a fervent heart.

So let us celebrate this radiant soul,

Whose passion for learning made her whole.

For in her journey, a lesson we find,

That beauty lies not in the surface, but in the mind

In the vicinity of stars, a constellation bright,

Shines a guiding light, forever in flight.

Her name, *Alika*, graces the cosmic stage,

A celestial being, a soul beyond age.

She possesses a magic, unique and rare,

An aura that sparkles, an enchanting flair.

With every step, she paints the world a new,

Infusing wonder in everything she pursues.

In her presence, time surrenders its hold,

As mysteries unfold, stories yet untold.

Her laughter, like stardust, sprinkles the air,

Filling hearts with joy, casting away despair.

Alika, a vessel of dreams and desires,

A whisper of inspiration, setting hearts on fire.

Her spirit soars with the wings of a dove,

Spreading love and kindness, a gift from above.

With words like poetry, she weaves a spell,

Weaving tales of wonder that forever dwell.

In her eyes, the universe finds its reflection,

A cosmos of beauty, an eternal connection.

Oh, *Alika*, you are a radiant star,

Guiding souls from afar, no matter how far.

May your journey be filled with magic and delight,

As you illuminate the world with your light.

In your presence, miracles come to be,

A testament to the power of dreams set free.

Alika, embrace the path that lies ahead,

For you are destined for greatness, it is said.

So let the universe sing your name,

As you continue to inspire, to rise above fame.

You are special, *Alika*, in every way,

A gift to this world, forever and a day.

In a world adorned with grace,

There shines a soul, a cherished face.

Her name, *Alika*, whispers on the breeze,

A symphony of beauty, her essence to appease.

Like a blossom in the morning light,

Her spirit dances, ever bright.

With eyes that hold celestial skies,

She paints a portrait, no art can surmise.

Alika, a beacon of strength and might,

Her presence, a constellation of pure delight.

With every step, she conquers the unknown,

A warrior's heart, a spirit of her own.

Her laughter, a melody that lifts the soul,

A river of joy, forever in control.

She weaves her dreams with threads divine,

Creating a tapestry, so truly fine.

In her embrace, warmth and solace reside,

A sanctuary where fears and doubts subside.

With gentle words, she nurtures the heart,

A healing balm, a masterpiece of art.

Alika, a symbol of love's grand design,

A symphony of compassion, so refined.

In your presence, life's colors bloom,

An eternal sun, dispelling the gloom.

May your journey be filled with endless delight,

Your dreams taking flight, reaching new heights.

Alika, may life's blessings unfold,

And may love's embrace forever enfold

Part II

A King's Arrival

Shah-The Last Independent Ruler.

In the divinity of ancient *Kashmir*'s tale,

Where *Sultan Chak* did prevail,

A warrior king, courageous and strong,

Defying odds, amidst conflict's throng.

The *Shahmiri* Dynasty's legacy grand,

Faced its end under *Habib Shah's* command,

Incompetent ruler, his reign did wane,

And *Chak* rose, a new path to attain.

This marked the *Chak* Dynasty's birth,

Gilgit-Hunza's Dard people, their worth,

They settled in *Kashmir*, land embraced,

Defying *Babur's* conquest, their honor encased.

Amidst these kings, *Shah* held its way,

The last native ruler, a noble display,

At thirty-five, the throne he did ascend,

In treacherous times, his strength he would lend.

In lands of old where legends thrived,

There stood a king, valiant and wise.

His name resounded through the realms afar,

Shah, the Knight King, a radiant star.

With armor gleaming, his heart aflame,

He rode with honor, his sword untamed.

A hero true, a beacon of might,

Shah wielded justice, his kingdom's light.

Born of noble blood, a regal birth,

Yet it was courage that defined his worth.

From humble beginnings, he rose with grace,

To claim his throne and rule the space.

In tales of yore, his valour renowned,

In every battle, his foes confound.

With every swing, his sword struck true,

Enemies faltered, their fears imbued.

In the darkest hours, when shadows fell,

Shah, undeterred, fought demons from hell.

He faced the tempests with unwavering stand,

A guardian bold, his kingdom's command.

A wise ruler, his subjects revered,

For *Shah*'s benevolence knew no bounds, it appeared.

He lifted the downtrodden, embraced the weak,

With empathy and kindness, his reign bespoke.

Yet *Shah* was more than just a king,

For his soul possessed a poet's ring.

His words flowed like a cascading stream,

Weaving tales of love, like a vibrant dream.

His knightly deeds were etched in lore,

But his heart's desires yearned for more.

For deep within his fortress walls,

Lay a longing for love that softly calls.

In distant lands, a fair princess dwelled,

Her beauty, a treasure, untamed and compelled.

Their destinies entwined, as fate decreed,

Two souls destined to fulfil love's creed.

Thus, in the pages of this epic tale,

Shah's journey unfolds, a grand travail.

As he traverses the realms, battles untold,

He seeks his love, a tale to behold.

So let us embark on this grand endeavor,

To witness the rise of *Shah*, the Knight King, forever.

Through trials and triumphs, love's path unwinds,

In a world where legends are forever enshrined.

In the company of Elysium, where legends abound,

A new chapter begins, with a resounding sound.

Shah, the Knight King, steps into the light,

A figure of strength, his presence ignites.

With the morning sun casting its golden hue,

Shah emerges, clad in armor anew.

His steed prances with fiery grace,

As he rides forth, determination on his face.

In a land untouched by mortal hands,

Shah seeks allies in distant lands.

His reputation precedes him far and wide,

A hero of valor, on whom many rely.

Through verdant forests and rugged plains,

Shah's path weaves, devoid of restraints.

His gaze sharp, his spirit aflame,

He journeys onward, seeking fortune's game.

From the towering mountains to the tranquil seas,

Shah's travels unveil hidden mysteries.

He encounters creatures of mythical lore,

Challenges faced like never before.

In a forgotten village, plagued by despair,

Shah arrives, a beacon of hope to repair.

He listens to their tales of sorrow and woe,

Vowing to protect them, his strength to bestow

With unwavering resolve, *Shah* takes command,

Uniting warriors, a courageous band.

Their swords held high, their spirits aligned,

They march forward, their purpose enshrined.

In the realm's heart, a malevolent force stirs,

Threatening to consume, chaos it prefers.

Shah, undaunted, leads the charge,

To face the darkness, his courage at large.

In battles fierce, his sword dances with grace,

Each swing a testament to his noble embrace.

He defends his people, their safety his creed,

A shield of righteousness, an unyielding lead.

But amidst the chaos, a soft voice whispers,

A melody of love, a tale that shimmers.

For *Shah*'s heart, burdened with honor and might,

Yearns for a companion, a guiding light.

As he traverses the realms, his eyes do meet,

A figure enchanting, with grace so sweet.

Their destinies intertwined, two souls collide,

In a realm where love's magic shall reside

A place where beauty finds its throne,

A verse to praise *Shah* must be sown.

Oh, let me sing of his grace divine,

A portrait of splendour, a love's design.

His visage, a masterpiece carved in stone,

Features chiselled, with strength they've grown.

Eyes, like stars, shine with noble might,

Reflecting depths that captivate the night.

His countenance, a symphony of charm,

With regal allure that could disarm.

A smile, warm as the sun's gentle rays,

Melting hearts with its radiant blaze.

His stature towers, like mountains tall,

Commanding respect, standing proud and tall.

Broad shoulders, a fortress of protection,

Embracing the world with noble affection.

But 'tis not mere form that makes him grand,

For within his heart, a love expands.

A beauty that transcends mere mortal gaze,

An essence pure, a soul ablaze.

His kindness blooms like flowers in spring,

A gentle touch, a healing it brings.

Compassion flows like a sacred stream,

Quenching thirsts, making spirits gleam.

His spirit, a tapestry of courage and might,

Brave and fierce, yet tender in sight.

With every battle, his valour aflame,

Championing justice, etching his name.

Oh, *Shah*, a sight to behold and adore,

A masterpiece painted on life's grand floor.

A symphony of beauty, both inside and out,

A King of grace, there's no doubt.

So let us raise our voices high,

In praise of *Shah*, the noblest sky.

May his beauty shine through realms untold,

A legend immortal, a tale to behold.

In his presence, hearts find solace and peace,

A beacon of hope, whose light will never cease.

With wisdom that guides, he leads with grace,

A sovereign revered, his realm's embrace.

His visage adorned with celestial light,

A countenance that shone through darkest night,

Eyes like orbs of precious gems, profound,

Reflecting wisdom, power unbound.

Golden locks cascading, a regal crown,

Touched by the gods, his splendour renowned,

With every step, he strode in noble stride,

Confidence and majesty by his side.

A voice that echoed, like a symphony's call,

Resonating through lands, both big and small,

Melodies of silk, enchanting and pure,

Entrancing all who heard, forevermore.

His armour gleamed, forged in the forge of fate,

A testament to strength, a warrior great,

In battle, he danced with swift precision,

Unleashing power, beyond all vision.

Legends whispered, of battles he'd won,

Against foes untamed, beneath the setting sun,

With each victory, his realm grew strong,

A testament to his valour, resolute and long.

But his true might lay not in the sword's might,

Rather, in compassion, burning bright,

For *Shah*, the last ruler, ruled with care,

Protecting his people, a kingdom rare.

He wove enchantments with benevolent hand,

Uniting hearts, across the land,

His reign a tapestry of peace and love,

Guided by wisdom from realms above.

Magical and mind-boggling, his reign unfurled,

A testament to a king who changed the world,

In tales and songs, his legend shall persist,

Shah, the last ruler, forever be missed.

So raise your voices, let the heavens hear,

The praises of a king, held dear,

Shah, the last ruler, our hearts doth sway,

In his beauty and valour, we find our way.

Part III

Hearts Intertwined

The Eternal Flame

Beneath the boughs of a *chinar* tree,

Alika's melodic voice danced free.

Her enchanting song, a symphony of grace,

Caught the heed of *Shah*, a noble embrace.

In the dappled shade, their paths entwined,

A fateful meeting, destiny designed.

For in that moment, two hearts did bind,

Alika, the queen, *Shah's* love enshrined.

She stood before him, a vision divine,

Radiant beauty that outshone sunshine.

Her words, like honey, caressed his ears,

Filling his soul with love's sweet veneers.

In her eyes, he found a realm untold,

A world of passion, of stories unfold.

Alika, the queen of his heart's domain,

Their love ignited, an eternal flame.

Together they walked, hand in hand,

A union of souls, a love unplanned.

She graced his court with regal might,

A queen in her essence, a radiant light.

In the chambers adorned with opulent art,

Alika reigned, captivating every heart.

Her wisdom surpassed the realm's demands,

Guiding *Shah's* rule with gentle hands.

In courtly dances and grand soirées,

Alika grace and charm set hearts ablaze.

Her presence elevated the empire's gleam,

A beacon of love, a shared dream.

Through trials and triumphs, their bond held strong,

A love that endured, where they both belonged.

Alika, the queen, by *Shah's* revered side,

Together they weathered the changing tide.

Their legacy etched in tales and lore,

A love story that time will forever adore.

Alika, the queen of *Shah's* sovereign domain,

Their love an immortal, everlasting reign.

In whispered echoes of the oral tradition,

Their love resounds, a cherished rendition.

Alika, the queen, in *Shah's* embrace,

A love story woven through time and space.

In a land where beauty reigns supreme,

There lived a *Shah* with a radiant gleam.

With handsome features and a courteous grace,

He captivated hearts, with a smile on his face.

Shah, a lover of music and art,

His soul danced to melodies, stealing his heart.

He sought the company of musicians and poets,

Their verses and songs, like soothing sonnets.

In his court, a symphony would unfold,

Where musicians played, their talents untold.

Strings were strummed, and flutes would sing,

Creating a melody fit for a lady love.

But among the performers, one stood apart,

A young maiden named *Alika*, with a gifted art.

Her voice soared high, like a *nightingale's* call,

Enchanting all who listened, both great and small.

Shah, bewitched by *Alika's* lyrical charm,

Found solace in her voice, a tranquil balm.

He'd sit in silence, as she weaved her song,

Transported to a realm where he truly belonged.

In the moonlit gardens, they often strolled,

Hand in hand, as their love gently rolled.

Alika's words, like poetry, touched his soul,

Creating a bond that only they could know.

Their love blossomed amidst the starlit night,

As *Shah* and *Alika* embraced with pure delight.

Their hearts entwined, a symphony divine,

Their union, an artwork, an eternal sign.

With the *Shah's* love for music and art,

And *Alika's* voice, a masterpiece impart,

Together they painted a tapestry of dreams,

Where love and beauty danced, like moonbeams.

So let their tale be whispered in every verse,

Of a *Shah* and *Alika,* blessed by love's curse.

For their story embodies passion's sweet sway,

Forever cherished, in the realm of music and clay.

In the heart of *Kashmir's* paradise,

Where *Dal Lake's* serenity does arise,

Their blossoms a love, pure and true,

Between *Alika* and her beloved, in a *Shikara's* view.

In a wooden boat, adorned with grace,

They navigate the tranquil embrace,

Each ripple in the water, a gentle kiss,

As they sail through the lake's eternal bliss.

Alika, a vision, with eyes like the moon,

Reflecting love, like a romantic tune,

Her laughter dances upon the shimmering waves,

A melody that even nature craves.

Beside her, her love, a soul intertwining,

In the *Shikara*, their hearts align,

With every stroke of the oar, a rhythm of desire,

Their souls entwined, their passion set afire.

They float on the mirror of pristine delight,

Under the stars, their love takes flight,

Whispering secrets to the night's sweet breeze,

They find solace in each other's ease.

As the moon's glow paints their world divine,

They pledge their love, a bond they'll enshrine,

Dal Lake bears witness to their sacred vow,

A union that will forever shine, somehow.

For in this realm of ethereal dreams,

Alika and her love find solace it seems,

Embraced by nature's majestic embrace,

Their love forever adorns *Dal Lake's* grace.

So let the waters of *Dal Lake* tell,

Of *Alika's* love, a tale they shall remember,

A story of two hearts that forever entwine,

In a *Shikara's* heaven, where love aligns.

In a world where love's sweet essence flows,

A tale of a couple, their love that grows.

Shah and *Alika*, a bond pure and true,

United in marriage, a love so imbued.

Like a radiant sun on a summer's day,

Their love blossomed, chasing worries away.

With hearts intertwined, they journeyed as one,

Their love story, a tapestry brightly spun.

From dawn to dusk, they showered love's embrace,

A tender symphony, a gentle grace.

With every sunrise and each twilight's hue,

Their affection deepened, their love ever true.

And in their love's garden, blessings did bloom,

Three precious souls, their joys to consume.

Their sons, a testament to love's sweet art,

An abundant love, etched within each heart.

The firstborn, a beacon of strength and might,

With laughter and courage, his spirit takes flight.

His dreams, vast as oceans, he fearlessly sails,

A vision of hope, his spirit never pales.

The second, a heart brimming with compassion,

In his caring embrace, a healing fashion.

With empathy's touch, he mends broken souls,

A refuge of solace, where love consoles.

The youngest, a spark, a light shining bright,

With curiosity's flame, he seeks endless height.

His mind, a wonderland of creativity's flair,

A muse of inspiration, beyond compare.

Together, the three, a triumphant trio,

Bound by a love that continues to grow.

Hand in hand, they embark on life's grand quest,

In each other's hearts, they find eternal rest.

Shah and *Alika*, their legacy's glow,

Nurtured by love, like a river's gentle flow.

Their sons, the embodiment of love's embrace,

A testament to their boundless grace.

May their journey be blessed with joy and cheer,

May love's melody serenade their every year.

In this tale of love, a family's delight,

Their story shines radiant, forever bright.

Both united, in a joyful embrace,

Alika and *Shah*, a family's tranquil grace.

Their love forged strong, their bond fortified,

A life of bliss, where happiness did reside.

With three precious sons, their world complete,

Laughter and love, a symphony so sweet.

United they stood, in life's gentle sway,

Unaware of the storm lurking in dismay.

But fate, a fickle weaver of life's design,

Sought to challenge the love they did enshrine.

A twist of events, an unforeseen test,

Their once sunny path, now shrouded in unrest.

Dark clouds gathered, casting shadows long,

Tears welled up, as their spirits grew strong.

Challenges emerged, like tempests untamed,

Threatening the love they had proudly claimed.

Yet, *Alika* and *Shah*, undeterred they stood,

Their love's flame burning bright as it should.

With hearts interwoven, they faced the storm,

Drawing strength from their love's unwavering form.

Hand in hand, they weathered the darkest nights,

Their love a beacon, shining steadfastly bright.

They leaned on each other, a pillar of strength,

Navigating the tempest's treacherous length.

For their sons, they fought, with unwavering might,

Protecting their dreams, like stars in the night.

In unity they stood, an unbroken wall,

Defying the odds, they would never fall.

Through the trials they faced, their love grew deep,

A bond unbreakable, even when shadows creep.

For fate may test, and luck may wane,

But their love's resilience would always remain.

Alika and *Shah*, an indomitable pair,

Their love, a testament, beyond compare.

Though fate may cross their path with twists and bends,

Their love's flame burns eternal, never to end.

In the meadows of Gulmarg, where beauty dwells,

A tale of love's fire forever swells.

Alika and *Shah*, souls entwined,

Bound by a love that fate designed.

A flame eternal, burning bright,

Illuminates the velvety night.

Amidst the *Kashmiri* paradise,

Their love blossoms, enchanting our eyes.

Like a sacred torch, their hearts ignite,

Flickering with passion, pure and right.

Through the seasons, their love shall endure,

In the meadows of Gulmarg, forever pure.

As the sun kisses the snow-capped peaks,

Their love kindles, never weak.

Through blossoming meadows, hand in hand,

They wander, as destiny had planned.

The fragrance of wildflowers fills the air,

As whispers of love caress with care.

Their laughter dances on the gentle breeze,

A symphony of love, embraced with ease.

The eternal flame they proudly bear,

A beacon of love, beyond compare.

Its radiance reflects in their eyes,

A love so strong, it never dies.

Through tranquil valleys and mountains high,

Alika and *Shah*, their spirits fly.

Their love, a tapestry woven divine,

An eternal flame, forever will shine.

In the meadows of *Gulmarg,* their love resounds,

A testament to love's sacred grounds.

May their journey be filled with bliss,

Forever blessed in love's eternal kiss.

Part IV

Shadow of Separation.

Separation

In the realm of anguish and woe,

Where hearts bleed and tears freely flow,

A tale of love and its bitter decay,

Unfolds with pain as night turns to day.

Alika, fair and full of grace,

Bound to *Shah*, in an eternal embrace,

Their love, once vibrant, now torn apart,

As destiny weaves its cruel, unyielding art.

The moon's soft glow, once their guiding light,

Now fades, obscured by an endless night,

Whispers of longing echo through the air,

As *Alika*'s soul, burdened with despair.

Through emerald meadows, they would dance,

Their laughter like melodies, a joyful trance,

But fate, cruel mistress, drew them apart,

Leaving a void that sears their fragile hearts.

Each day a tempest, ravaging their souls,

As memories haunt, and pain takes its toll,

Alika's tears, like rivers, endlessly flow,

For *Shah*, her love, who she can no longer know.

In dreams, their love thrives, a vivid bloom,

Yet waking hours reveal the painful gloom,

The ache of absence, a relentless sting,

As their spirits yearn for a mending spring.

The stars, once witnesses to their devotion,

Now seem distant, lost in the vast ocean,

Alika, now adrift, her spirit broken,

Yearning for the words yet unspoken.

In a realm where love once bloomed so bright,

Now comes a tale of separation's blight.

Alika and *Shah*, two souls entwined,

Bound by love, but destiny unkind.

Their hearts once danced to love's sweet tune,

A harmony that echoed 'neath the moon.

Their spirits intertwined, forever bound,

A love that seemed eternal, profound.

But alas, the winds of fate conspire,

To test their love, to fuel the fire.

Circumstances cruel, tears them apart,

A chasm carved within each heart.

Alika, a vision of grace and light,

Her absence now a starless night.

Her laughter, once a symphony so clear,

Now fades away, a distant echo to hear.

Shah, the Knight King, his spirit worn,

In solitude, his heart is torn.

Aching for the touch he now can't find,

Yearning for the love he left behind.

Oh, the pain of separation's sting,

Like thorns that pierce, cruel and unforgiving.

Distance stretches, a vast expanse,

Their souls reaching out, but caught in a trance.

Each passing day, a moment lost,

A void that deepens at love's high cost.

Their memories, like bittersweet wine,

Both a comfort and a torment, intertwined.

Yet even in the face of such despair,

Their love's flame flickers, still aware.

For in their hearts, a glimmer remains,

A bond unbroken, through life's trials and pains.

They hold on to hope, with steadfast belief,

That destiny's plan will grant them relief.

For love, though tested, can conquer all,

And bring together what once did fall.

So let us wail for *Alika* and *Shah,*

Separated souls, entangled in a mar.

But let us also believe in love's might,

That in time, their paths shall reunite.

For in the realm of love's eternal grace,

True love endures, no matter the space.

And as their story unfolds, we shall see,

If love's true power can set them free.

In the gardens of *Nishat*, where blossoms bloom,

Lies a tale of love, of heartache, and gloom.

Alika, fair maiden with eyes of twilight,

Her essence, a fragile rose in the moonlight.

Her spirit danced in the fragrant air,

Amidst the whispers of love and despair.

Her laughter, a melody that enchanted the skies,

A symphony of joy, her soul's lullabies.

But fate, cruel mistress, had other plans,

For *Alika* and her love in distant lands.

A suitor adorned with wealth and power,

Promised her a life in a gilded tower.

Yet *Alika's* heart, it beat for another,

A humble poet, a soul like no other.

In the quiet corners of *Nishat's* embrace,

They shared stolen moments, a clandestine grace.

Their love, a flame burning fierce and bright,

Ignited their souls, alight in the night.

But jealousy's venom, it slithered and seeped,

As rumours spread, secrets unveiled, hearts wept.

The moon witnessed their tear-stained embrace,

As *Alika* departed, leaving no trace.

Her footsteps echoed in *Nishat's* hollows,

As the poet's sorrow drowned in sorrow.

Now *Nishat's* gardens are painted in gray,

For *Alika's* absence stole colors away.

Her memory, a thorn in every petal's bed,

A haunting ghost, a love story left unsaid.

Oh, *Alika,* a heart wrenched in timeless pain,

In *Nishat's* embrace, love shall remain.

For your spirit still dances among the flowers,

Etched in verses, whispered in moonlit hours.

In the realm of *Mughal's* glory, a tale I bring to thee,

Of *Alika* and her lover, bound by love's decree.

A lyrical ballad, woven with anguish and despair,

As *Akbar's* tyranny prevailed, their love caught in its snare.

Alika, a radiant soul, adorned with grace and might,

Her lover, a valiant warrior, his spirit shining bright.

But *Akbar,* the emperor, with his iron fist of reign,

He deemed their love forbidden, a fire he would tame.

He cast his judgment swiftly, with no remorse or heed,

Imprisoning the warrior, sowing sorrow like a seed.

In the tower of shadows, he languished day and night,

While *Alika* wept in solitude, her heart got blight.

Oh, *Alika* fair, in the depths of your despair,

Your love, like a wild river, flows beyond Akbar's snare.

With courage in your veins, and fire in your eyes,

You embarked on a quest, to free your love from ties.

Through treacherous paths and moonlit starry skies,

Alika braved the perils, her spirit never dies.

She rallied loyal souls, with hearts true and bold,

To challenge *Akbar's* rule, and the story yet unfolds.

With swords gleaming bright and rebellion in their cries,

They stormed the palace gates, defying *Akbar's* lies.

But destiny, fickle mistress, had a different course in sight,

As *Alika* approached, her lover vanished from her sight.

Akbar, cunning as a foe, had played a wicked game,

He moved his captive warriors, leaving her lover wanted.

Yet, undeterred, she had a heart that still believed,

In a love that could conquer all, if only it was received.

Oh, *Alika*, valiant and true, your song shall never fade,

In the annals of history, your love's story will be displayed.

For love's flame cannot be quelled by any prison cell,

It transcends the earthly realm, where souls forever dwell.

So raise your voice, oh troubadours, let the *balad* be sung,

Of *Alika* and her lover, whose hearts were tightly strung.

Though separated by tyranny and a merciless decree,

Their love, a beacon shining bright, for all eternity.

In the valleys of *Harmukh Pass*,

Where nature's beauty held steadfast,

There dwelled a love, like none surpassed,

Between *Alika* and her lover, cast.

With eyes as bright as stars above,

Alika's heart knew naught but love.

Her lover, strong with valour's might,

Stood tall, a beacon in her sight.

But fate, cruel mistress, took her toll,

And cast upon them a somber role.

For deeds misunderstood and unjust,

Alika's lover was sent to the dust.

Behind cold bars, his spirit confined,

His heart, entangled, left behind.

But *Alika*, with unwavering grace,

Vowed to bring light to this darkened space.

She painted dreams upon the wall,

A tapestry of hope for one and all.

Through letters, her love found its way,

To the depths of his soul, day by day.

With every verse she penned and sent,

Alika's love grew fervent.

In words, she wove a tapestry so grand,

It bridged the gap across the land.

She whispered of the fragrant breeze,

And of the mountains, majestic trees.

Of moonlit nights and starlit skies,

And how love within their hearts still lies.

Through her words, she painted scenes,

Of freedom found in cherished dreams.

She spun tales of love's enduring flame,

Igniting hope, though freedom tame.

In *Harmukh Pass*, where shadows fall,

Alika's love defied the prison's thrall.

She dreamed of the day when he'd be free,

Together, embracing destiny.

And as the seasons came and went,

Alika's love remained unspent.

Till one fine day, with joy untamed,

Her lover's release, the world proclaimed.

United once more, in love's sweet embrace,

They stood together, face to face.

Their spirits strengthened, their love restored,

Through hardship, trials, and much more.

For in the depths of *Harmukh's* domain,

Alika's love conquered pain.

Through letters penned and hearts entwined,

Love's eternal flame forever shined.

In the realm of love's lament, she roamed,

Alika, the poet with her heart bemoaned.

Her king, once near, now distanced and apart,

Left her soul adrift, seeking solace in her art.

Through the meandering paths, she wandered free,

With verses etched upon her memory.

Her melodious voice, a *balm* to her pain,

She sang the songs of separation, the refrain.

In every corner she sought, in every breeze,

Yearning for the touch that put her heart at ease.

Her voice, like a gentle river's flow,

Carried the echoes of longing as she'd go.

Her words, like petals, fell upon the air,

Whispering tales of love and deep despair.

Each verse a vessel for her yearning soul,

As she strayed, seeking to make herself whole.

Through bustling markets and deserted streets,

Alika's voice resounded, its power and heat.

The crowds would gather, drawn by her song,

Transfixed by the emotions that flowed along.

Her voice, a vessel for her love's plight,

Sang in separation, in the day and night.

The moon would listen, casting its soft glow,

As *Alika's* voice traversed high and low.

In gardens blooming with fragrant delight,

She sang of longing under starlit night.

Her voice, a beacon in the darkest hours,

Expressing love's pain through dulcet powers.

With every word that danced upon her lips,

She wove a tapestry, the heartache eclipsed.

Her songs, a testament to love's great cost,

Echoed through valleys, where hearts were lost.

And as she wandered, searching for her love,

Her voice soared high, like a lone mourning dove.

Alika, the poet, renowned and revered,

Through her songs, love's essence persevered.

Though the path was long, she stayed resolute,

Her voice, a vessel for her love's pursuit.

And in her journey, she found strength anew,

As love's melodies carried her love's residue.

Through every city, village, and distant shore,

Alika's voice resonated, forevermore.

For in her wandering, love's power was revealed,

As her voice and heart became forever sealed.

Part V

Echoes of Soliloquy

Harmony's Embrace

In the depths of sorrow, *Alika* stood,

Her love's departure, a pain that could

Shatter her world, leave her all alone,

In penury and destitution's zone.

Once adorned with love's tender grace,

Now she dwelled in a desolate space,

Her heart bereft, aching with despair,

Fragile and broken, beyond repair.

Gone were the days of warmth and delight,

Replaced by shadows, an endless night,

No whispered words, no comforting touch,

Only echoes of love that meant so much.

Her home, once filled with laughter's cheer,

Now echoed emptiness, loneliness near,

The walls stood silent, no joy resounds,

Her hopes shattered, dreams scattered on grounds.

The world moved on, oblivious to her plight,

While she battled demons, day and night,

In penury's embrace, she found her place,

Struggling to survive, a forgotten face.

Her once adorned garments, tattered and worn,

A poignant symbol of how she was torn,

By life's cruel twists, its relentless blow,

Reduced to scraps, the depths of woe.

With empty pockets, hunger as her friend,

Her spirit tested, it seemed to no end,

But within her, a flicker of strength remained,

A resolve to rise, not to be restrained.

For in adversity, she found her might,

A phoenix emerging, ready to fight,

With determination as her guiding light,

Alika, in penury, would reclaim her right.

Through resilience and a resilient heart,

She would rebuild, piece her life's shattered part,

Destitution may bind her for a while,

But her spirit's flame would surely reconcile.

For *Alika*, though left alone in despair,

Would rise above, her burdens to bear,

Her journey through penury's dark expanse,

Would lead her to a newfound stance.

A beacon of hope amidst trials untold,

A testament to the human spirit bold,

In her rise from destitution's grip,

Alika would find strength in every hardship.

So let this poem be a tribute to her,

In penury's realm, a survivor,

May her story inspire those who face,

The depths of life's challenges, their own grace.

In the land of beauty, where tales unfold,

Lived a soul adorned with words untold,

Alika, the Nightingale of *Kashmir's* lore,

A poetess divine, her spirit did soar.

In the tapestry of time, her verses wove,

With ink of passion, her emotions strove,

Her words, like pearls, gleamed with grace,

A poetic symphony, her soul's embrace.

Her heart, a canvas of colors profound,

Painting emotions in verses unbound,

With unmatched verbal prowess she sang,

A melody of words, like a silver tang.

Through the valleys and mountains high,

Her poems echoed, touching the sky,

Like gentle breezes, they whispered along,

Captivating hearts with their rhythmic song.

Alika, in her solitude's retreat,

Found solace in words, her heart's beat,

With ink as her companion, she would dwell,

In realms of verse, where stories would swell.

Her verses carried the fragrance of the rose,

And the pain of love that forever flows,

Each word a treasure, carefully penned,

A testament to the depths she would transcend.

In her poetic realms, she found solace rare,

An escape from life's burdens, a tender air,

Through pen and paper, her soul would fly,

A sanctuary of words, where dreams lie.

Oh, *Alika, the Nightingale of Kashmir's* embrace,

Your poetry transcends time and space,

With every verse, you touched souls deep,

A legacy of beauty, forever to keep.

May your words resonate through ages vast,

Inspiring hearts, for eternity to last,

A poetess revered, your spirit we cherish,

Alika, the Nightingale, forever nourished

In the valley's embrace, *Alika* found her truth,

A nightingale with melodies to impart,

A soul awakened, guided by the root,

She embarked on a quest to touch each heart.

With wings unfettered, she soared through the air,

Her song, a beacon in the twilight's gleam,

A symphony of love, beyond compare,

A tale of ascetic life, her chosen theme.

Amidst the emerald meadows, she did roam,

A nomad seeking solace, far and wide,

Her voice, a river, in melodic tome,

Unleashing depths of beauty, far inside.

From mountaintops to valleys deep and low,

Alika's songs of freedom gently flow.

Through sacred forests and serene retreats,

Alika's song, a testament, repeats.

In realms where dreams take flight and passions soar,

There dwells a soul named *Alika*, forevermore.

Once bound by love's embrace, a heart entwined,

Now blossomed, divine, a poetess of the mind.

In separation's veil, where tears may fall like rain,

She turned to pen and paper, her solace to attain.

From sorrow's depths, she rose with grace and might,

A phoenix, born anew, her words now taking flight.

Oh, *Alika*, poetess of radiant verse,

Your spirit now unleashed, in every line immersed.

With ink as your ally, and dreams as your guide,

You dance upon the pages, where emotions coincide.

As divinity of knowledge graced your very being,

You wove enchanting stories, like whispers worth seeing.

Each syllable a gem, adorned with heartfelt pain,

In every stroke of pen, your wisdom would sustain.

From the depths of longing, you crafted tales untold,

With metaphors of love, more precious than gold.

Your verses danced like stars, adorning night's attire,

And in the reader's heart, they set their souls on fire.

The universe rejoices, as your name takes flight,

A poetess renowned, a beacon shining bright.

Through separation's sorrow, you found destiny's role,

To heal tender words, and make broken hearts whole.

So, *Alika*, embrace your divinity of the pen,

For your words shall resonate, again and again.

May your verses touch the heavens and the earth,

A testament to love's enduring worth.

In this tapestry of life, where stories intertwine,

You've become a legend, forever etched in time.

Oh, *Alika*, divine poetess, may your journey be grand,

As you traverse the realms of wisdom, hand in hand.

Part VI

Silent Demise

Shadows of a fallen *Shah*

In the realm of darkness, where whispers reside,

Lies the tale of a fallen *Shah*, with shadows as his guide.

A lament unfolds, of death's cold embrace,

And the pain that lingers in this desolate space.

Once, a sovereign of opulent reign,

His glory eclipsed the sun's golden domain.

But fate, cruel mistress, played her wicked part,

And toppled his throne, shattering his heart.

The echoes of his kingdom, mere whispers in the night,

As the shadows dance, casting their eerie light.

They whisper of battles lost, of blood-soaked ground,

And the shattered dreams that no solace has found.

Oh, fallen *Shah*, your legacy tarnished and stained,

By the hands of destiny, so cruelly ordained.

Your empire crumbled, like castles made of sand,

Leaving naught but sorrow and grief in its command.

The shadows weep, for they bear witness to the pain,

Of a once-mighty ruler, now shackled in disdain.

They mourn the lives lost, the cries of despair,

As death's icy fingers claimed what was once fair.

In the corridors of power, where ghosts silently weep,

The fallen *Shah*'s spirit forever etched, forever to keep.

His shadowed presence haunts the darkest of nights,

A tragic reminder of life's relentless plights.

Yet, amidst the sorrow, a glimmer of hope may rise,

For tales of fallen heroes often find solace in the skies.

De Memory of the *Shah* finds peace in time's gentle breath,

And may the shadows of his legacy find solace in death.

In this melancholic dirge, the shadows unfold,

A lament for a fallen *Shah*, a tale of death and pain untold.

May his spirit find solace, released from sorrow's plight,

And his memory be enveloped in a forgiving, eternal light.

In a land where love's flame did ignite,

A tale of *Shah* and his beloved *Alika*, so bright.

Their hearts entwined, a celestial sight,

But destiny weaved a bittersweet plight.

Shah, a prince with valour and grace,

Alika, a beauty with an enchanting face.

Their souls entangled in love's embrace,

Bound by a passion no one could erase.

But fate's cruel hand did intervene,

Separating them, a heart-wrenching scene.

Alika, torn from *Shah*, their love unseen,

A tragic twist that left their hearts unclean.

Shah, in anguish, wandered the night,

His heart weighed heavy, stars his only light.

He yearned for *Alika*, his soul's true plight,

Longing for her presence, her touch so right.

Through valleys and deserts, he searched afar,

Every step driven by his love, a shining star.

Seeking his *Alika*, no matter how far,

He vowed to reunite, to erase the scars.

Days turned to nights, and nights to days,

As *Shah's* love for *Alika* burned ablaze.

His spirit resilient, he followed love's maze,

Guided by hope, in its mystical haze.

At last, he found her, in a distant land,

Alika, his love, standing hand in hand.

But fate, once again, dealt a cruel hand,

Their reunion tainted by an unseen strand.

Alika, upon her lips, a final breath,

Leaving *Shah* broken, lost in love's death.

He held her close, as she succumbed to the depths,

A separation etched in their souls, till the last breath.

In grief, *Shah* wept, his heart torn apart,

The pain of separation piercing like a dart.

But their love, immortal, would forever chart,

A tale of devotion, engraved in every heart.

In the realm of love, *Shah* and *Alika* reside,

Their story a testament, forever unified.

Separation may have claimed their earthly stride,

But love's essence, unbroken, forever tied.

And so, their tale shall echo through time,

A love eternal, a flame that won't decline.

Shah and *Alika*, entwined in love's chime,

A bond unbroken, a love so divine.

War clouds loomed, *Mughals* sought revenge,

For past defeats, their anger did impinge,

Finally, they launched an assault,

But *Shah's* resistance could not be fault.

Brave *Kashmiri's* rallied, undeterred,

Against the invaders, their courage stirred,

Though outnumbered, they fought with might,

Their homeland's freedom, their eternal right.

The *Mughals*, cunning, sought a deceit,

Inviting *Shah* for talks, discreet,

Against counsel, he journeyed to *Agra's* shore,

Never to return, his fate would be more.

Akbar, the Emperor, imprisoned the king,

In *Agra's* confines, sorrow's sting,

Years in captivity, his spirit unwavering,

His people's plight, his heart still engraving.

Exiled to *Bihar*, a *jagir* bestowed,

Yet destiny's path, with hardship flowed,

Forced to join *Mughal* conquest afar,

In *Orissa's* battles, a distant star.

Jagat Nath Puri, the place of his demise,

At last, a Sultan's spirit flies,

Shah the warrior, a legend's end,

Kashmir's native king, forever commend.

Amidst the mountains, his valour remains,

In the annals of time, his story sustains,

A poem to honour his noble name,

Shah, eternal in fame.

In the depths of sorrow's embrace, a tale unfolds,

Where the *Shah* departed, his reign untold.

Every soul carried whispers of despair,

And in distant *Kashmir,* anguish filled the air.

Alika, the queen, her heart shattered and torn,

Her spirit, once vibrant, now with grief adorned.

Her tears, like rain, washed the valley's face,

As sorrow echoed in every sacred space.

In the land of serene beauty, pain took hold,

And the mountains wept, their stories untold.

The *chinar* trees mourned, their leaves turned to rust,

For a beloved ruler turned to fleeting dust.

Oh, *Kashmir*, wounded soul of the land,

Your valleys weep, your mountains stand,

In the wake of a ruler's tragic demise,

Your heartache echoes beneath azure skies.

The rivers flowed, carrying tales of woe,

As the people's lament, like a gentle blow,

Echoed through the *Dal*, through every meadow,

A requiem for a kingdom lost in shadows.

The saffron fields, once vibrant and gold,

Now cloaked in sorrow, their essence untold.

The lotus weeps upon the shimmering lake,

For a noble reign now bound by fate's ache.

But amidst the pain, resilience takes flight,

The people of *Kashmir*, brave and bright,

Gathered their strength, as stars filled the night,

To forge a new path, with hope as their light.

Through the mist of agony, a new dawn emerged,

United they stood, their spirits surged,

For in the depths of sorrow's cruel sting,

The seeds of resilience began to sing

Oh, *Alika*, mourned queen of *Kashmir*'s land,

May your tears nourish, where hope now stands.

In the tapestry of grief, let healing threads weave,

A tale of rebirth, where love will never leave.

So let this poem be a vessel of pain,

A testament to *Kashmir*'s enduring reign.

For even in anguish, beauty finds a way,

To guide the spirit towards a brighter day.

In the realm of *Kashmir*'s tale so grand,

After *Shah*, a shift of hand.

Agony engulfed its scenic land,

A history veiled in sorrow's demand.

Mughals arrived with their mighty force,

Subduing the valley on their course.

Kashmir became a prized resource,

Its destiny entwined with a new source.

Afghans, they came, a brief interlude,

But *Sikhs* emerged with power imbued.

They conquered the land with warrior fortitude,

Kashmir's fate yet again renewed.

Dogra rule dawned, a century-long reign,

Gulab Singh's empire, a dominant chain.

Yet shadows of suffering did remain,

As history etched scars with lasting pain.

British shadows cast upon the land,

Their influence, a manipulative hand.

Kashmir, caught in a foreign command,

Bound by ties that none could withstand.

Partition's flames engulfed the sky,

Choices made, tears in every eye.

Amidst the chaos, a question: why?

Kashmir's destiny left to defy.

Conflict erupted, hearts torn apart,

The struggle for *Kashmir*'s beating heart.

Wars waged, lives shattered from the start,

A tale of anguish, tearing worlds apart.

Laws that were made were, a fragile shield,

But the winds of change refused to yield.

Autonomy stripped, wounds unhealed,

Kashmir's story, in agony concealed.

Through valleys and mountains, whispers persist,

Of a land yearning for peace, not clenched fist.

May understanding and harmony persist,

To soothe the agony that can't be dismissed.

In *Kashmir*'s tale, a longing remains,

For a future where tranquillity regains.

A history shaped by enduring pains,

Yet hope lingers in its poetic refrains.

Epilogue

The Legacy of Eternal Love

In the wake of *Shah* and *Habba Khatoon* passing, their love story continued to reverberate through the ages, leaving an indelible mark on the hearts of all who heard it. The world mourned the loss of these extraordinary souls, yet their legacy endured, eternally woven into the tapestry of time.

Their departure left a void, but it also ignited a spark of inspiration in those who had been touched by their love. Their story became a beacon of hope, a reminder that even in the face of mortality, love transcends all boundaries and lives on forever.

The pages of history turned, carrying with them the echoes of *Shah* and *Habba Khatoon* love. The world continued to spin, and their tale evolved into a symbol of enduring devotion, an emblem of the power of connection that stretches beyond the realms of life and death.

Their love became a source of solace for those who faced their own trials and tribulations. The story of *Shah* and *Habba Khatoon* reminded them to persevere, to embrace love in all its forms, and to cherish the fleeting moments that make life meaningful.

Generations came and went, yet the memory of *Shah* and *Habba Khatoon* remained alive, passed down through whispers and retellings. Their love became a cherished legend, woven into the cultural fabric of the land they once called home.

Monuments rose in their honour, castles dedicated to love's unwavering spirit. People from far and wide made pilgrimages to these sacred sites, seeking solace, guidance, and a glimpse into the immortal love that *Shah* and *Habba Khatoon* had shared.

Artists painted their portraits, poets composed verses in their honour, and musicians crafted melodies that evoked the depths of their love. Their essence transcended mere mortal existence, becoming an eternal muse for those seeking to capture the essence of love's grandeur.

In the hearts of those who truly understood, *Shah* and *Habba Khatoon* lived on as an eternal flame, an embodiment of the transformative power of love. Their love story became a reminder that love, when nurtured and cherished, becomes a force that reverberates across time and space.

And so, dear reader, as you close the final chapter of this book, remember the tale of *Shah* and *Habba Khatoon*. Let their love inspire you to embrace the fleeting moments, to cherish the connections that grace your life, and to leave behind a legacy of love that transcends the boundaries of mortality.

For in the grand tapestry of existence, it is love that weaves us all together, connecting souls across time and space. May the legacy of *Shah* and *Habba Khatoon* be a guiding light, illuminating your own journey and reminding you that love, in all its infinite forms, is the true essence of life itself.

Thank You